PIANO • VOCAL • GUITAR

# THE LIGHTER SIDE OF
# CHRISTMAS

ISBN 0-634-01822-1

HAL•LEONARD®
CORPORATION
7777 W. BLUEMOUND RD. P.O. BOX 13819 MILWAUKEE, WI 53213

Visit Hal Leonard Online at
**www.halleonard.com**

# C O N T

E N T S

# ALL I WANT FOR CHRISTMAS IS YOU

Words and Music by MARIAH CAREY
and WALTER AFANASIEFF

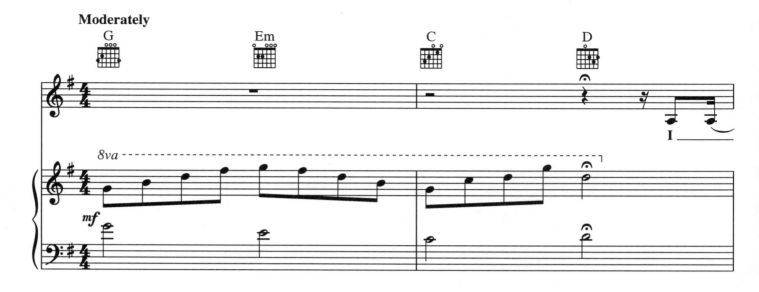

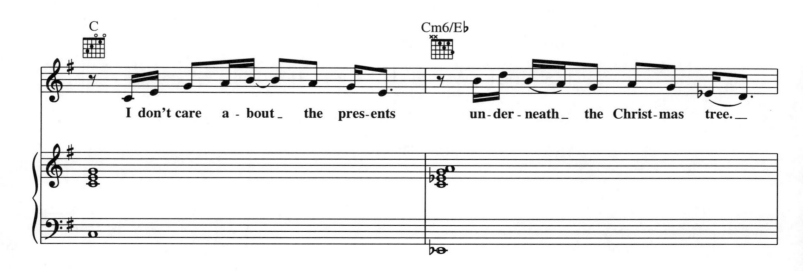

I just want you for my own, more than you __ could ev - er know.

Make my wish come true: __ all I __ want for Christ - mas is you, __

Moderately fast

yeah. __

# FELIZ NAVIDAD

Music and Lyrics by
JOSE FELICIANO

# FROSTY THE SNOW MAN

Words and Music by STEVE NELSON
and JACK ROLLINS

# GOIN' ON A SLEIGHRIDE

Words and Music by
RALPH BLANE

ice and snow.\_\_\_\_ We've got a com-fort, A fan-cy quilt-ed

com-fort, If we hit a lit-tle storm it's gon-na keep us warm.\_\_\_\_

Ev-'ry-bod-y's go-in', Hearts are o-ver flow-in', Start your har-mo-

niz-in', that's a full moon ris - in';

# GOIN' ON A DATE WITH SANTA

Words and Music by
RANDY BROOKS

# GRANDMA GOT RUN OVER BY A REINDEER

Words and Music by
RANDY BROOKS

**Moderately bright**

Grand-ma got run o-ver by a

rein-deer　　walk-ing home from our house Christ-mas Eve.

You can say there's no such thing as San-ta,　　but as for me and Grand-pa, we be-

lieve.

1. She'd been drink-ing too much egg-nog
2., 3. *(See additional lyrics)*

and we begged her not to go, but she for-got her med-i-

ca-tion, and she stag-gered out the door in-to the snow.

When we found her Christ-mas morn-ing at the scene of the at-

You can say there's no such thing as San-ta, but as for me and Grand-pa, we be-

lieve. _____

*Additional Lyrics*

2. Now we're all so proud of Grandpa,
   He's been taking this so well.
   See him in there watching football,
   Drinking beer and playing cards with Cousin Mel.
   It's not Christmas without Grandma.
   All the family's dressed in black,
   And we just can't help but wonder:
   Should we open up her gifts or send them back?
   *Chorus*

3. Now the goose is on the table,
   And the pudding made of fig,
   And the blue and silver candles,
   That would just have matched the hair in Grandma's wig.
   I've warned all my friends and neighbors,
   Better watch out for yourselves.
   They should never give a license
   To a man who drives a sleigh and plays with elves.
   *Chorus*

# GRANDMA'S KILLER FRUITCAKE

Words and Music by ELMO SHROPSHIRE
and RITA ABRAMS

The hol-i-days were up-on us and things were go-in' fine, 'til the day I heard the door-bell and a chill ran up my spine. I

I winced at Wil-ma's giz-zard mousse, but

said it tast-ed fine. But that leth-al wea-pon

Grand-ma baked is where I draw the line. _____ It was

**D.S. al Coda**

**CODA**

cake! It's ear-ly Christ-mas morn-in'; the

# GRANDPA'S GONNA SUE THE PANTS OFFA SANTA

Words and Music by RITA ABRAMS,
ELMO SHROPSHIRE and JON GAUGER

doubt you can re-mem-ber Grand-ma's pass-ing, that trag-ic, mourn-ful tale so of-ten
day while griev-ing Grand-pa watched the T V, he heard some ad-ver-tis-ing law-yers

sung. The prime sus-pect is one of San-ta's rein-deer, in the
swear they'd win a mul-ti-mil-lion dol-lar set-tle-ment and

# THE HAPPIEST CHRISTMAS

Words by MILES RUDGE
Music by TED DICKS

# HAPPY CHRISTMAS, LITTLE FRIEND

Lyrics by OSCAR HAMMERSTEIN II
Music by RICHARD RODGERS

The soft morn-ing light of a pale win-ter sun is

trac-ing the trees on the snow. Leap up lit-tle friend and

fly down the stairs for Christ-mas is wait-ing be-low. There's a

# HAPPY HOLIDAY

## from the Motion Picture Irving Berlin's HOLIDAY INN

Words and Music by
IRVING BERLIN

mer - ry bells keep ring - ing, may your ev - 'ry wish come

true. Hap - py hol - i - day, _____ hap - py

hol - i - day. _____ May the cal - en - dar keep

bring - ing hap - py hol - i - days to you.

# A HOLLY JOLLY CHRISTMAS

Words and Lyrics by
JOHNNY MARKS

# HOW LOVELY IS CHRISTMAS

Words by ARNOLD SUNDGAARD
Music by ALEC WILDER

How love-ly is Christ-mas with boughs in the
love-ly is Christ-mas when chil-dren are

hall, when bells rin-gle jin-gle and friends come to
near, the sound of their laugh-ter, sweet sea-son of

call. How love-ly is Christ-mas with joy on the
cheer. How love-ly is Christ-mas with gifts by the

# IT'S BEGINNING TO LOOK LIKE CHRISTMAS

By MEREDITH WILLSON

# I GUESS THERE AIN'T NO SANTA CLAUS

Music by BARRY MANILOW and EDDIE ARKIN
Lyric by JOHNNY MERCER
Additional Lyric by BARRY MANILOW

I got wine, __ I got cheer. I got no - bod - y here. I

*D.S. Instrumental solo*

guess there ain't no San - ta Claus. ___ Well, they

sure ___ got it right when they sing "Si - lent Night." I

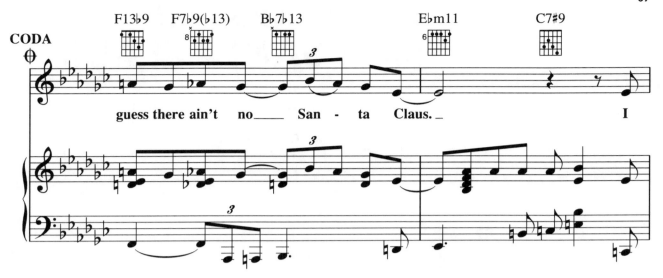

**CODA**

guess there ain't no___ San - ta Claus.___ I

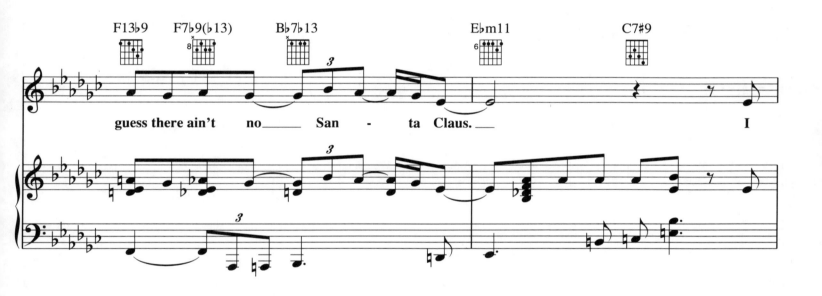

guess there ain't no___ San - ta Claus.___ I

**Freely**

guess, guess there ain't no San - ta Claus.___

# I SAW MOMMY KISSING SANTA CLAUS

Words and Music by
TOMMIE CONNOR

# I'VE GOT MY LOVE
# TO KEEP ME WARM

from the 20th Century Fox Motion Picture ON THE AVENUE

Words and Music by
IRVING BERLIN

# IT MUST HAVE BEEN THE MISTLETOE
## (Our First Christmas)

By JUSTIN WILDE
and DOUG KONECKY

# IT'S A WONDERFUL CHRISTMAS THIS YEAR

Words and Music by MARIE LESTER
and TIM HAYDEN

It's a won-der-ful Christ-mas this year

as we fill it with hol-i-day cheer. The

# JINGLE-BELL ROCK

Words and Music by JOE BEAL
and JIM BOOTHE

# LET IT SNOW

Words and Music by WANYA MORRIS
and BRIAN McKNIGHT

# JINGLE, JINGLE, JINGLE

Music and Lyrics by
JOHNNY MARKS

Moderately, Gaily

# LET IT SNOW! LET IT SNOW! LET IT SNOW!

Words by SAMMY CAHN
Music by JULE STYNE

Moderately

Oh, the weath-er out-side is fright-ful, but the fire is so de-light-ful, and since we've no place to go, let it snow! let it snow! let it snow!

It does-n't show signs of stop-ping, and I
fi-re is slow-ly dy-ing and, my

# MERRY CHRISTMAS, BABY

Words and Music by LOU BAXTER
and JOHNNY MOORE

**Slow Blues**

*Instrumental solo ad lib. (2nd time only)*

# THE MERRY CHRISTMAS POLKA

Words by PAUL FRANCIS WEBSTER
Music by SONNY BURKE

Moderately (Tempo di Polka)

# MERRY MERRY CHRISTMAS, BABY

Words and Music by MARGO SYLVIA
and GIL LOPEZ

# A MERRY, MERRY CHRISTMAS TO YOU

Music and Lyrics by
JOHNNY MARKS

*Use any language desired.

(*) Can repeat full chorus then 4 bar vamp shouting languages, then Coda.

# MISTER SANTA

Words and Music by
PAT BALLARD

2. Mister Santa, dear old Saint Nick
   Be awful careful and please don't get sick.
   Put on your coat when breezes are blowin',
   And when you cross the street look where you're goin'.
   Santa, we (I) love you so,
   We (I) hope you never get lost in the snow.
   Take your time when you unpack,
   Mister Santa don't hurry back.

3. Mister Santa, we've been so good
   We've washed the dishes and done what we should.
   Made up the beds and scrubbed up our toesies,
   We've used a kleenex when we've blown our nosesies.
   Santa look at our ears, they're clean as whistles,
   We're sharper than shears
   Now we've put you on the spot,
   Mister Santa bring us a lot.

# NUTTIN' FOR CHRISTMAS

Words and Music by ROY BENNETT
and SID TEPPER

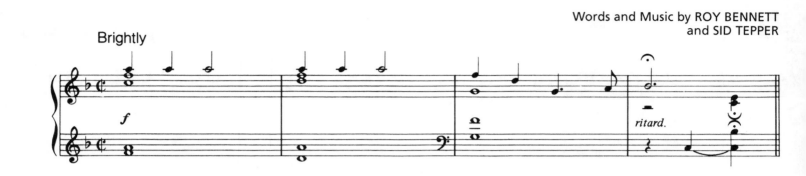

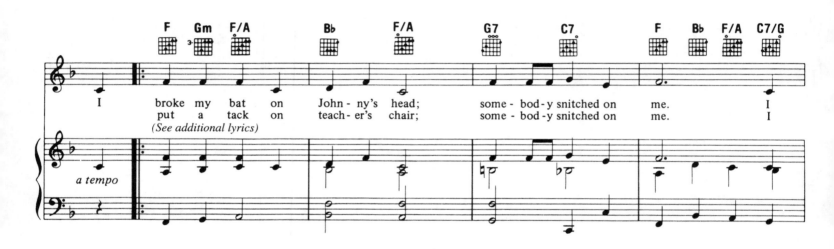

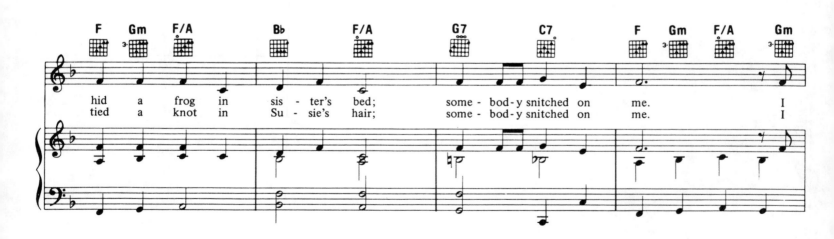

3. I won't be seeing Santa Claus; somebody snitched on me.
He won't come visit me because somebody snitched on me.
Next year I'll be going straight, next year I'll be good, just wait,
I'd start now but it's too late; somebody snitched on me. Oh,

# PINE CONES AND HOLLY BERRIES

## from HERE'S LOVE

By MEREDITH WILLSON

# ROCKIN' AROUND THE CHRISTMAS TREE

Music and Lyrics by
JOHNNY MARKS

# SANTA BABY

By JOAN JAVITS, PHIL SPRINGER
and TONY SPRINGER

# RUDOLPH THE RED-NOSED REINDEER

Music and Lyrics by
JOHNNY MARKS

**Moderately fast**

You know Dash-er and Danc-er and Pranc-er and Vix-en,

Com-et and Cu-pid and Don-ner and Blitz-en, but do you re-

call the most fa-mous rein-deer of all?

# SANTA, BRING MY BABY BACK
## (To Me)

Words and Music by CLAUDE DeMETRUIS
and AARON SCHROEDER

Bright rock

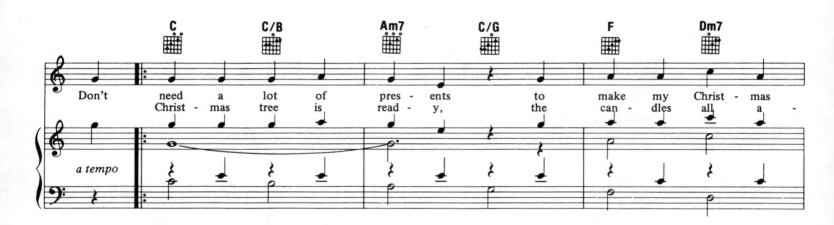

# SANTA CLAUS IS BACK IN TOWN

Words and Music by JERRY LEIBER
and MIKE STOLLER

Christ-mas time, pret-ty ba-by, and the snow is fall-in' on the ground.

You be a real good lit-tle girl, 'cause San-ta Claus is back in town.

'cause San-ta Claus is back in town.

(Christ-mas,) (Christ-mas,) (Christ-mas.)

# SHAKE ME I RATTLE
## (Squeeze Me I Cry)

Words and Music by HAL HACKADY
and CHARLES NAYLOR

# WHEN SANTA CLAUS GETS YOUR LETTER

Music and Lyrics by
JOHNNY MARKS

# SUZY SNOWFLAKE

Words and Music by SID TEPPER
and ROY BENNETT

# THAT'S WHAT I'D LIKE
# FOR CHRISTMAS

Words and Music by LESLIE BRICUSSE
and CYRIL ORNADEL

**Bright Waltz**

# WONDERFUL CHRISTMASTIME

Words and Music by
McCARTNEY